P9-APA-860

Understudies

- **Written by John Parsons**
- **Illustrated by Nicola Belsham**

Contents	Page

Rigby

Understudies

With these characters ...

Mr. Hogget

Walter

The
Conductor

Maurice and
Misha

"The sho

Setting the scene ...

Mr. Hogget, the new owner of the old Majestic Theater, has managed to persuade the world-famous Misha and Maurice from France to perform the world's most famous ballet—in his theater!

With the help of Mr. Hogget's assistant, Walter, the Majestic Theater has been transformed to its former glory. The angels are sparkling with a new coat of paint, the orchestra is tuned up, and the rehearsals have been magnificent. Nothing can go wrong . . . or can it?

῀ must go on!"

Chapter 1.

From the outside, the dark old Majestic Theater looked haunted. The theater had not been used for fifty years. It had towering marble columns on either side of the entrance. They were badly cracked and seemed as though they were about to topple over.

Above the doorway, there were
angels carved into the stone.
Once, the angels had been painted
in glittering gold, but now the paint
was peeling. Only the noisy pigeons
roosting in the rooftop seemed to
appreciate this rundown old theater.

Inside the theater, something was happening. A shaft of light could be seen coming from underneath an office door. The office door was marked "Stage Manager." From behind the door, someone could be heard talking excitedly and shuffling papers.

After fifty years with no shows and no music and no dancing, someone had bought the old Majestic Theater. Exciting plans were being made to restore the old theater to its original condition.

Stretched out in his shiny new leather chair, Mr. Horace Hogget, the new owner, had a big grin on his face. He hung up the phone, clapped his hands, and dialed his assistant. After a few rings, a voice said, "Hello?"

"Walter," said Mr. Hogget. "I've done it!"

"Done what?" said Walter.

"I have booked the great Misha and Maurice to perform the world's most beautiful ballet for our opening night!" said Mr. Hogget proudly. "We'll have enormous crowds! We'll have the newspaper and television reporters here. We'll have a full house every night for a week! We'll be successful!"

"Are you sure you've got the right Misha and Maurice?" asked Walter suspiciously. "The world-famous Misha and Maurice from France?"

"Absolutely," replied Mr. Hogget. "They're coming to our town on vacation, and I've convinced them to help us out!"

"Misha and Maurice at the Majestic," said Walter slowly. "I can't believe it!"

"Rehearsals start in three weeks," said Mr. Hogget eagerly. "So let's get this theater restored. We need builders, electricians, painters, and cleaners. We need advertising, press releases, and TV and radio coverage. We need posters. We need cold drinks and snack food. We need an orchestra. And Walter," said Mr. Hogget.

"Yes," said Walter.

"The entrance must look spectacular. Those columns and angels need a thorough cleaning after fifty years of pigeons living above them. And please buy a can of glittering gold paint. Hurry! We've got a lot of work to do!"

Chapter 2.

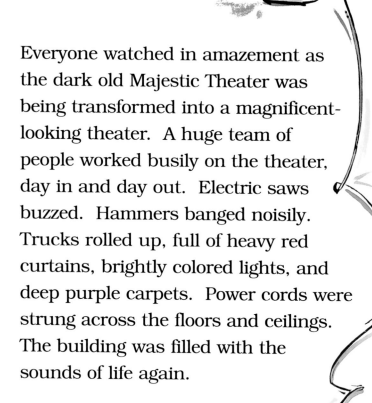

Everyone watched in amazement as
the dark old Majestic Theater was
being transformed into a magnificent-
looking theater. A huge team of
people worked busily on the theater,
day in and day out. Electric saws
buzzed. Hammers banged noisily.
Trucks rolled up, full of heavy red
curtains, brightly colored lights, and
deep purple carpets. Power cords were
strung across the floors and ceilings.
The building was filled with the
sounds of life again.

The columns were scrubbed down until they were gleaming. The angels sparkled and shone in their bright new coat of glittering gold paint. The pigeons fluttered about nervously.

One week before opening night, the two world-famous ballet dancers arrived. Misha and Maurice rehearsed their leaps and twirls, day after day, while the orchestra rehearsed the music—plucking, drumming, and blowing until everything was just perfect.

Mr. Hogget beamed as he wrote press releases and faxed them off to every newspaper, radio station, and TV newsroom in the country. The town was covered in posters announcing this major event. All the hotels became full, as reporters arrived from the city to cover the biggest story in town: the grand opening of the Majestic Theater.

At last, after three weeks of preparation, the night of the dress rehearsal came around. The members of the orchestra, resplendent in their black dresses, suits and bow ties, took their places. The lighting crew huddled high above the stage, with hundreds of switches, levers, and knobs all lit up and ready to go. Mr. Hogget and Walter sat eagerly in the front row waiting for the rehearsal to start.

The conductor tapped his baton on the music stand. It was his signal for the orchestra to begin to play. Misha and Maurice swept onto the stage in their magnificent ballet costumes.

The final rehearsal had begun.

When it was over, Mr. Hogget leapt to his feet and clapped loudly. He had tears in his eyes.

"That was magnificent, marvelous, *magnifique!*" he exclaimed. "That was the most majestic ballet I have ever seen."

He went up to Misha and Maurice and shook their hands.

"Everything is perfect," he said. "And to celebrate, I would like you to join Walter and me for dinner! Tomorrow night, you will be our superstars!"

That night at dinner, Maurice and Misha smiled, nodded, and ate everything on their plates. Ballet dancers needed a lot of energy food! Mr. Hogget and Walter were too excited to eat anything. Instead, they just talked and talked and talked about how the restored Majestic Theater was about to become the most famous theater in the country!

Little did they know that they were right.

Chapter 3.

Opening night was clear and bright, with the moon shining down on the golden angels. Mr. Hogget sprang up the steps of the theater two at a time, whistling cheerfully. He strode into his office and sat down in his shiny leather chair, looking very pleased with himself. Walter was waiting for him, beaming with excitement.

"All seats have been sold out for a week," said Walter.

"Every dance and drama critic in the country is staying in town," added Mr. Hogget.

"Everything is cleaned, polished, vacuumed, and ready to go," said Walter.

"Nothing can go wrong," said Mr. Hogget, beaming.

But then it did.

The phone on Mr. Hogget's desk rang, and he picked up the receiver.

"Allo?" came a French voice on the phone. "Zis is Maurice ere."

"Allo!" said Mr. Hogget. "I mean, hello!"

"We ave a disaster," said Maurice. "We ave ze allergy to something in ze food. We ave eaten something bad last night. Misha and I—we cannot leave ze hotel. All we can do is groan and go to ze bathroom! Now, ze ballet dance is . . . is . . . impossible!"

Mr. Hogget's face turned gray.

"But the theater . . . the tickets . . . the TV and the radio . . . the show must go on!" he stammered into the phone.

"I'm sorry," said Maurice. "It is impossible. And now I must go to ze bathroom again. I must go to ze bathroom very fast!" The phone clicked and the line went dead.

Mr. Hogget's face turned red. Then it turned purple. Then it turned white.

"I'm ruined!" he cried. "It's a disaster!"

Chapter 4.

Outside, crowds had waited to watch the rich and famous people arriving for the show. Famous dance and drama critics from newspapers, TV, and radio waved as they walked slowly up the steps, making sure that the cameras were aimed in their direction. They liked to think that they were almost as famous as the performers themselves!

"Of course, the show will be a failure if I don't like it," sniffed one newspaper critic as a TV reporter interviewed her.

"I have, as you know, seen every show — good and bad," added another, as he adjusted his bow tie for the newspaper photographers.

"I expect that this show won't be anything special," sighed a famous TV host, as he waved at the crowd.

Inside his office, Mr. Hogget sat slumped with his head in his hands. Walter coughed nervously as he fidgeted with the show's program.

"I suppose I had better tell everyone the show is off," he said. "We'll be laughed at by everyone, but there's nothing we can do."

Mr. Hogget made a low grumble. It turned into a long growl. Then he stood up, looked Walter straight in the eye, and banged the desk with his fist.

"I will not let the audience down!" he said firmly. "The show must go on!"

"But . . ." said Walter, looking anxious.

"NO BUTS!" roared Mr. Hogget. "Take off your shoes and come with me!"

Chapter 5.

Inside the theater, a hush fell across the audience. The lighting crew adjusted the buttons and knobs and levers, and the theater went dark. The conductor tapped his baton, and everything was silent.

Then, in a blaze of colored lights, and with a great fanfare from the orchestra, the red curtains rose.

The audience gasped.

A short, fat figure appeared in a ballet costume so tight it looked like the seams would burst. He wobbled across the stage and bowed. A tall, thin figure in a ridiculous-looking frilly tutu did a very awkward curtsy. Both dancers were red-faced and looked scared. The conductor looked alarmed, and the entire orchestra turned around to see what was happening.

"PLAY!" hissed the short, fat ballet dancer. The conductor waved his baton and the orchestra started to play.

The audience started to giggle. Mr. Hogget and Walter thumped from side to side of the stage. They flung their arms around in time with the music. They spun each other around until Walter lost his grip and went crashing noisily off the stage. The audience laughed. After a series of wild twirls, going around and around and around, Mr. Hogget got very dizzy and wobbled around the stage.

When Walter's short, frilly tutu ripped and got tangled up in his ballet shoes, the audience roared with laughter and cheered. Mr. Hogget slid across the stage on his knees, arms wide apart, and almost appeared to fly as he shot right off the stage and into a shocked violin player. The audience clapped and clapped and called for more.

Finally, the curtain fell, and the orchestra breathed a sigh of relief. The audience swarmed outside onto the theater's steps and chatted excitedly about the show.

"That was the most entertaining dance I have ever been to," said the first newspaper critic.

"It was the first time I didn't fall asleep during a ballet," nodded the other critic. "A very clever modern-dance style."

"I want those guys on my show," demanded the famous TV host.

Backstage, Mr. Hogget wiped the sweat from his forehead. Walter looked unhappily at the bruises starting to appear on his sore elbows and throbbing knees.

"I think we did OK!" said Mr. Hogget.

"They seemed to like it," said Walter. The conductor rushed in.

"It was an enormous success," he cried. "You should hear what they're saying outside!"

"Really?" said Walter. "Well, I did think my twirls were rather good. I think we should go out to dinner to celebrate!"

Mr. Hogget glared at him.
"Dinner to celebrate?" he scowled. "NO WAY! A dinner to celebrate got us into this mess in the first place!"

"The show must go on!"

Hogget bought the theater Majestic
With performers booked and rehearsals fantastic
The theater transformed amazingly quickly
When suddenly the performers became sickly.

The food they ate brought on an allergy
It looked as though it would all end in tragedy
All they had worked toward, all going wrong
When Hogget declared, "The show must go on!"